Dedication

To my daughters, Madison and Jordan, thank you for being the inspiration for this book and for teaching me how to be a mom.

To my son, Justin, for bringing a completeness to my role as a mom before I even knew something was missing.

And to my son, Tom, for letting me experience the friendship that can come after the main role of "mom" is done.

Table of Contents

Preface

I am lucky enough to be a mom of four children, but I will genuinely admit that it is my daughters I am most worried about in today's world. My sons have an advantage their sisters do not...simply, their Y chromosomes. There are societal, cultural, and yes, even biological, differences which will make many aspects of life easier for my sons. My daughters will have to fight for positive recognition on traits that their male classmates will be rewarded for (bossy, outspoken, aggressive, ambitious). They will continue to experience societal double standards. They will eventually have to fight harder for equal pay and for leadership positions. They will have the pressure of deciding whether to have children. They will face the traditional societal prejudice if they decide not to get married, and the modern societal prejudice if they decide to be stay-at-home wives or mothers. In short, they and their female counterparts, will experience more challenges than their male peers.

As I reflected on my daughters' lives, I began to think about my own and the lessons and experiences I have acquired throughout my life. So many of my own lessons were things that I heard from others, although I may not have taken the sage advice when it was given and only in retrospect, and after some pain or hardship, would it make sense. So when I thought about writing a book for my daughters, I asked myself why I would limit it to just my one, limited perspective? My mom frequently stated the adage, "It takes a village to raise a child", so I decided to ask people in my life - friends, colleagues, family members - to share their advice. I started a simple question on email, and was amazed at the response. The wealth of insight and, more touching, the willingness to share such personal thoughts left me humbled. I began to wonder what might happen if I reached out to strangers and when I did, the same thing happened. Whether people sitting next to me on planes, or people I met in restaurants, or colleagues at professional functions, or while doing lunch duty at my kids' schools, or people responding to my online survey, people from all over the world offered their advice for teenage girls. Their words are offered as they were written; none have been edited for content to ensure their true voices are heard. The result is a collection of insights, stories, suggestions and advice collected originally for young women, but truly a catalog of thoughts for anyone whether as a personal reflection, or a "reset button" for future inspiration.

Ultimately, though, *Voices from the Village* is for young women preparing to enter a world which is not always fair and which is challenging, and to do so with the collective support of those who are already members of the Village...people who were willing to share their personal experiences to create this book. Do I believe that it will help girls avoid all the mistakes of those who came before them? No, but if each girl who reads this book takes just a few pieces of advice away and incorporates them into her personal narrative, then maybe it can help her avoid some of the mistakes some of us have made. Or maybe it will help her realize that others have experienced the same struggles. And maybe she will realize that the things she has heard from her parents are not just from her "overprotective" or "nagging" parents, but advice others have for her as well. Maybe some of the advice will resonate at times when things are overwhelming. Or when she has to make a choice between the easy path or the hard path. Maybe it will help her know that there is a world of people out there who understand and support her, even when she may not be supporting herself. And maybe, she could use this book as a guide throughout the years leading up to adulthood, and the initial years of her indoctrination into the Village as an adult.

- Robin

BODY

"There is nothing more rare, nor more beautiful, than a woman being unapologetically herself; comfortable in her perfect imperfection. To me, that is the true essence of beauty."
— *Steve Maraboli, Unapologetically You: Reflections on Life and the Human Experience*

"This is a call to arms. A call to be gentle, to be forgiving, to be generous with yourself. The next time you look into the mirror, try to let go of the story line that says you're too fat or too sallow, too ashy or too old, your eyes are too small or your nose too big; just look into the mirror and see your face. When the criticism drops away, what you will see then is just you, without judgment, and that is the first step toward transforming your experience of the world."
— *Oprah Winfrey*

"Beauty shouldn't be about changing yourself to achieve an ideal or be more socially acceptable. Real beauty, the interesting, truly pleasing kind, is about honoring the beauty within you and without you. It's about knowing that someone else's definition of pretty has no hold over you."
— *Golda Poretsky*

Stop worrying about what your body looks like and focus on what your body can do for you.
– Lisa, 37

Wear a helmet.
– Matt, 40

Do yoga; it is a way to learn to love and appreciate your body.
– Anonymous

Take care of your body; it's the housing to everything you are. Eat healthy, exercise, wear sunscreen, get enough sleep, and don't sweat the small stuff. Do all these things, and love the body that you've been given. Don't compare it to others. We all buy products to better ourselves, but think twice before you do. Challenge yourself to NOT buy the latest product with your hard earned allowance, job earnings, etc....and save it for something big that would be really special to you.

– Darlene, 34

Eat what you love in moderation. Skinny doesn't matter, healthy matters.

– Melissa, 44

Remember as a woman you own your body and no one can demand to have it; it is a gift you choose to give.
– Lesley, 67

Use a good face cream,
daily,
now.
– Erin, 42

Whatever negative image or feelings you have right now, you will not always feel this way.
– Anonymous

Eat well,
> sleep well,
>> take your vitamins.
>>> – Terri, 51

Take a self-defense course and don't be afraid to practice what you learn.
– Modia, 40

> God gave you your body,
> so love it as much as you love God.
>> – Anonymous

Respect yourself, but don't worry about whether other people like you for the way you look; other qualities are far more important.
– Len, 44

Practice sexual abstinence at any cost until you are married.
– Modia, 40

Listen to your body and your mind. Never do something to please someone else. You are your own person and a good friend/boyfriend would never force you to do something you're not comfortable doing.
– Gina, 24

You are already beautiful. Work to enhance your internal beauty, and your external beauty will follow suit.
– Don, 73

Barbie is not a real person.
– Quinton, 45

Wear sunblock everyday.
– Mary, 64

Eat less; move more.
Go easy, very easy, on salt, sugar, and fat
(think *vegetables*).
– Don, 73

Never.

     Never.

          Never tattoo anyone's name on your body!

You are not property to be branded.
- Tom, 45

Don't feel you have to be in a hurry to have sex, but if/when you feel you are ready BE INFORMED, practice safe sex, and don't be in a hurry to start a family, before you've finished your education, or before you even know what you want to do with your life.

– Len, 44

Appreciate your body and your face at each stage of life rather than critiquing it; you'll wish for what you have now when you're older.

– Robin, 42 (as shared by her dear friend, Leona)

Respect yourself, and don't let others define or influence who you are and what you do, including alcohol, drugs or sexuality.
– Arnie, 61 ("but feels 39")

Having a 24 inch waist isn't going to make you a better person.
– Jenn, 39

Avoid bad habits like drugs, tobacco or alcohol, because they are neither healthy nor necessary for a good social life; besides, you'll also spend a lot less money, and be less dependent on others for your happiness.
– Len, 44

Learn to love yourself and your own inner and outer beauty. Find your own style and develop it. The media is full of what young women are supposed to look like and young women try so hard to fit in. If I could wave a magic wand for young women it would be to love themselves enough to be themselves.
– Sandy, 67

Abstain/practice safe sex.
– Mary, 64

First of all, even if you are an early bloomer and seem to have all the attributes of a grown woman, don't worry...you aren't done yet. If you feel that you aren't beautiful, focus on health. If you get proper exercise and nutrition, your body will arrange itself into an aesthetically pleasing shape. If you have proper nutrition, your hair will get thicker and shinier. Underage drinking (especially binging), illegal drug use, smoking, and living on chips and energy drinks will show on you. Making your health your #1 priority now will give you a good foundation now for beauty throughout your life.

– Denise, 43

I would want her to understand her mind and body as the only, precious ways she can experience life. We all have only our own fragile selves to carry us through a lifetime of experience. She will have to protect and strengthen her mind and body in order to be up to this amazing opportunity. By being the strongest and healthiest she can be, she will be able   to   do   almost   anything!
- Joli, 51

Take technology seriously. Don't ever take a pic of yourself (video) that is compromising. It will come back to haunt you. You never know whose hands it will land in.
– Lisa, 37

It will take you a while to find the clothes and fabrics that fit your body right, look good on you, and that you can afford. The "figuring it out" process can stink but build your wardrobe piece by piece and don't delete pictures of you in your old wardrobe. It'll show you how far you have come in discovering your style/fit...plus it's always good to have a laugh.

– Trish, 37 ("although some days I feel like I'm 14")

Devote yourself to a hobby/sport that keeps you physically active. It will start you on a path to keep you active as you age.

– Andrea, 51

Try not to see the images of women presented in ads (magazine, TV, etc.) as real. They are highly directed and photoshopped and do NOT represent reality.
– Mari, 44

From a relationship perspective, cherish your beautiful body, learn everything you can about it, and only share it with someone who truly loves you and respects you. And when you do decide to share your body with someone, help that person learn your body, speak up for what you want and what makes you feel good. If your partner loves you and values you, they will listen and learn. Your physical interactions should be reciprocal; not one sided. If you're not able to vocalize this to your partner, then you're not ready to move past hand holding.
– Darlene, 34

Stay active in sports. DON'T quit when your body starts to change or when you get better at sports than the boys. It's OK to be smarter, faster, and better at sports than boys.
– Mary, 64

Do not text and drive - for that matter, you should avoid even using the phone for conversation while you're behind the wheel, unless it's
hands-free.
– Len, 44

My kids are all tall. They take after their daddy's side of the family. My sister's daughters were also tall. She used to tell them to wear short heels so they wouldn't tower over the boys in their class. I don't remember saying anything to my girls about their height, but people would always say, "My, she's tall!" And I'd say, "Yep, just like her dad! AND she is so sweet and generous, too." Embrace who and what God made you. You are perfect. As you grow older, you figure out that when it comes down to it, people who matter to you and who you matter to, don't care what's on the outside as long as you are good hearted and honest and kind.

– Anonymous

Be involved in extra curricular activities and stay active.
— Gina, 24

Take good care of yourself. Exercise by doing something
you enjoy: ride a bike, shoot a basketball,
take a neighbor's baby for a walk.
— Anonymous

Always respect your body; it is a gift from God.
— Laura, 50

Always be true to yourself.

Just be you.

You are beautiful.

Enjoy your life.

– Anonymous

Remember the grass isn't always greener. In high school, there was a girl who was so skinny and could eat whatever she wanted. One day she was complaining about not being able to keep weight on. I said, "I wish I had that problem". Without missing a beat, she said, "And I wish I could have calves that looked like yours." I thought, "Really??" But as someone who was so thin, she wanted a body that had some muscle to it. I remember that day as a turning point of being happier for what my body can do for me.

– Lisa, 37

HEART

Only in Relationship can you know yourself,
not in abstraction and certainly not in isolation.
– J. Krishnamurti

Love. Fully and honestly.
Even if it hurts sometimes, you deserve to know
what love feels like.
- Laura, 28

Use your beauty and uniqueness to help others.
– Jim, 49

I would advise girls to be inclusive of all - to put themselves
in the shoes of those who may be less popular than them
or likely to be bullied –
and make every girl and guy feel special.
– Leslie, 48

A person you are attracted to and interested in romantically may be a wonderful person but if your life long goals don't line up is probably not the life long person for you.
– Elisabeth, 47

Boyfriends come and go but true girlfriends are forever. High school will soon be a speed bump in your rear view mirror.
– Jennifer, "old-enough-to-be-wiser"

Make, cherish and nourish your friendships. Never lie - especially to yourself. Do something nice for yourself and for someone else everyday.
– Anonymous

Family first.
– Anonymous

Know you can do it on your own –

buy a house,

raise your kids,

pay your bills,

travel,

get the car fixed,

paint a room,

hire a repairman,

all of it.

Because if you know you can do it, you won't pick a person because you NEED someone, but because you WANT that one.

- Deanna, 53

Surround yourself with positive people, always have a go-to person (preferable your mom) and if you can't say it in front of your grandmother you probably shouldn't say it.
– Jayne, 49

It is great to meet a boy you like, but do not make him number one and leave out your girlfriends. Always keep your girlfriends. Girlfriends are girls who treat you with respect and treat you how you would like to be treated, and you do the same for them. Girlfriends are friends you trust, confide in, care about, people who help you in need and you want to help when they are in need and you expect nothing in return.
– Laura, 50

Remember your parents love you, but they don't know how
to be parents. So cut them some slack.
– Terri, 51

Words from my father helped me many times while
growing up but a few stuck with me. When feeling insecure
or inadequate, he would tell me not to compare myself with
others. I might always find a girl smarter, more athletic,
more popular but she would never be "more" at everything.
He would remind me that even the girl who seemed so
perfect had weaknesses, too, just like me.
– Lee, 43

Sometimes, you don't need a reason or an excuse to do the
thing that heals your heart.
- Laura, 28

Love your parents even when they drive you crazy.
– Gina, 24

Be a change agent in this world leaving behind good
memories in people's lives.
– Modia, 40

Appreciate your parents, you may not see it now, but they are right.
- Anonymous

Love yourself and others will also love you. Stay true to what you believe in even if the rest of the crowd doesn't follow you. In the end they will come to realize you were right.
– Elizabeth

Include your parents in your life. They love you like you couldn't even begin to imagine. It doesn't take a lot to make your parents your allies. Take 5 minutes a day to ask how their day was. Tell them one or two good or bad things that happened to you each day or two. This builds a respect and appreciation for what your daily life is like. Most parents don't want to control your life; they just want to be a little part of it.
– Anonymous

Friends must earn your friendship.
– Modia, 40

I would want a girl to treat herself as her own, most loved, best friend. Give herself good advice, and listen to it, trust it and take it to heart. You would never give careless or bad advice to someone you love, so care about yourself in that way.
- Joli, 51

It's hard to love someone if you don't love yourself.
– Chelsey

We all want to be respected, but are we respected by all?
– Jerry, 67

You may not think so now, but mom is right!
– Sue, 67

Know that even though you may think your little brother/sister is a pain in the neck, in the end they will look up to you and the decisions you are making and will use that information as they make decisions.

– Sue, 67

Friends make the best relationship partners.
– Tom, 45

It doesn't matter whom you date or even whom you marry; they only absolutely binding contract is with the person with whom you have a baby.
That's one no piece of paper can end.
– Elisabeth, 47

First, the truism: Do unto others as you would have them do unto you.

Then the kicker: Rid yourself of others who do not treat you the same way.

– Don, 73

Of all the BFF's you have now, only a small fraction will
remain important later in your life.
– Quinton, 45

Boys are not worth the trouble they cause. Find some
friends who love you the way you are, and work to keep
that friendship strong.
– Melissa, 44

I would encourage her to align herself with friends and
acquaintances who are going her way, in a positive
direction for life accomplishments.
– Rita, 67

Don't ever stay in a relationship (with friends, boyfriends)
where you are treated poorly;
you deserve better.
– Tina, 45

Embrace differences. Everyone is special.
– Elizabeth

Never trust strangers.
– Tim, 55

Listen to the voice inside you, even - and especially - when
it goes against what the group is doing.
– Kelli, 42

Help your parents with household chores every day. You'll get their assistance with a lot less effort whenever you want something from them.
– Anonymous

You know how it hurts your feelings when someone teases or makes fun of you? Remember that when you're tempted to pick on someone else.
– Sara, 36

It really is not embarrassing to be seen with your parents.
Cherish the time you have with them.
– Ron, 72, and Betty, 65

Do not lie to your parents, regardless of the situation.
They will help.
- Phil, "at the peak of middle age, and about 25-30 years from
retirement"

If you are feeling anxiety about your relationships, write down the 20 names of people who are most important to you AND giving you stress: you wished they liked you and they don't, you are afraid they will stop liking you, that sort of thing. Exclude immediate family members. Now look at that list. In the next 3-6 years, you will lose contact (aside from an occasional Facebook "like") with half the people on that list. In 10-15 years, you will probably only ever think of or have contact with 2 or 3 people on that list, and they probably won't be important to you anymore. In 25 years, if you ran across this list, you would not really remember who some of these people were, and you'd be shocked that some of the people on the list were anyone you ever considered important. Now go back to the top of your list and write your own name. I guarantee you, you will never lose contact with that person or forget about her, and her opinion will always matter. Don't make decisions to please others on that list if they conflict with your values, needs, or goals.
– Denise, 43

People who matter will love you for who you are
on the inside.
– Jenn, 39

Whatever issues you may have with friends and classmates,
differences and disagreements always seem worse than
they actually are.
– Anonymous

You are not better than anyone and no one is
better than you.
– Michele, 42

Keep your mother and sisters close. That unique female
bond will be critical later in life. It is a relationship that
can't be replicated.
– Lynne, 59

Be open and honest with your mom. Your mom is your best friend and she will get you through the hardest and toughest times. The more open and honest you can be with your mother, the hardest situations don't always seem too bad.

– Lauren, 20

There are a lot of idiots!
– Maureen, 12

In a day and age where it is so easy to be brought off track by peers and social situations, technology and social media, ALWAYS take care of you and be safe! Respect yourself (even when others don't). Have the strength to say, "No!" and walk away from any person or situation who isn't good for you. One moment or experience can change your life forever and not always for the better. What you put online is there FOREVER. Always consider the long-term ramifications of your "networking".

– Stephanie, 39 ("or 21")

Dating that person you just met or stare at in class but
never spoke to before is exciting
and most often short lived.
– Tom, 45

It gets better, because if junior high and high school are the
best years of your life, there is something wrong.
– Kelli, 42

As much as it feels like it...the teen years are NOT forever!! People grow up...the girls, or boys, who are tormenting you now, will soon be just a memory. Yes, it's drama filled, but it's not the rest of your life...the path becomes clearer, and easier to follow.

– Jenn, 39

Stay true to yourself, even when others might try to convince you otherwise.

– Erin, 42

Do yourself a favor and don't try to be everyone's friend.
Friends come and go throughout our lives and it is
important to always have one TRUE friend that gets you,
understands you and loves you no matter what. Find that
one good friend you can grow old with and be the best
friend you know how to be. Don't ditch her once you have
a boyfriend or girlfriend; they come and go, too.

– Anonymous

Spend lots of time with your family and if your parents
seem busy, tell them you need them. Mother, father, sibling
whatever, but family time is good.

– Denise, 42

Listen to your mother.

— Marty, 56 ("but I don't act or look like it")

You are not a maid. Do not allow boys to ask you to pick up after them.
- Anonymous

Be smart, kind and thoughtful; model this, especially to younger girls.
— Anonymous

Boys are only a distraction, and are not worth it....take as much time to figure out who you want to be and what you want to do before you even think about getting into relationships, and you will be happier in the long run because of it.
– Melissa, 32

Words hurt and, if it comes from your mouth, be strong enough to say you are sorry. Sometimes words and quiet actions such as rumors, notes written, texts and emails sent secretly are shared and it can be painful. Choose your words well; be honest, with other's feelings in mind.
– Laura, 50

Trying to be nice to everyone will make you more real friends than trying to be popular.
– Tom, 45

Limit those you can truly trust to very few (those you can
count on one hand). Trusting too many with too much
personal information can end up hurting you later.
– Ron, 72, and Betty, 65

The best thing you can do when you get married is to be
sure you have great girlfriends. Not just at the wedding but
as a second support system. Your partner will be your
partner but your friends knew you before you fell in love.
– Trish, 37 ("although some days I feel like I'm 14")

Thank you notes/emails are the most powerful
tool in the world.
– Anonymous

Take pictures and actually print them out. Hang them around you in your home, car, wherever.
– Anonymous

Know the people that care about you (10 times out of 10, it's family) and turn to them for advice; they truly have your best interest at heart.
– Gabrielle, 19

Pay attention to what you think of you, not what others think of you. Nurture, respect and love yourself first before you love someone else.
- Kristen, 42

Everyone is a little awkward as a teenager. Everyone -- except the upper echelon 10% of beautiful patricians of popularity. Trust me, they won't be so cute at your ten-year high school reunion. BUT, you know what else will happen at your reunion -- everyone will be human again and nice. Teenage years are chemical-filled spurts of angst, growth, and raging against imagined (and some real) injustices. They seem like they last forever.

> *But they don't.*
> *They pass.*
> *Then the real fun starts.*
> – Jen, 33

Remember that the people you date in high school aren't supposed to be the people you marry. While it is easy to imagine building a life with this person you are in love with, it is also important to remember that you are only a teenager. You are going to learn a lot and grow a lot after the age of 18. So, if you are dating someone and it doesn't work out...it is going to be okay. If you are dating someone and you don't like how they are treating you, break it off. Someone better will come along. Consider high school a practice run for when you are living on your own and truly ready to meet someone who will be a great life partner.

– Amy, 46

I encourage girls to make friends. Just because people look, speak, act, dress, are in different classes or have different interests than you, this does not mean that they could not be wonderful people with great personalities who would brighten or add to your world.

– Kristin, 27

Moms are good for you - yes they are! They were there once; mind you they will probably tell you to do the opposite of what they did because now they know"ish" better. But they also know that by making mistakes you can sometimes learn the biggest lessons.

– Kara, 32

Let the people you love know it.
– Mary, 64

Enjoy your loved ones.

My grandparents would visit every Saturday night and as a teen, I went out with my friends instead. What I wouldn't do now to go back in time and spend a Friday night with them verses some lame boy.
– Lisa, 37

Respect your parents, but realize that you are your own person, and your own goals, dreams and habits do not need to match theirs.
– Len, 44

Value your relationships with your family and remember they love you always and only want the best for you although sometimes you might not feel that way.
– Laura, 50

Try counting to five before you respond to someone who is driving you crazy. You may avoid some fights, some tears, some really hurtful words, some lies and overall a ton of unnecessary bad feelings.
– Kara, 32

Be appreciative of your partner.
　　Every day,
　　　　every minute,
　　　　　　every breath.
　　　　　　– Trish, 37 ("although some days I feel like I'm 14")

If you are in a relationship and the person you are in love with (or friends) limits you or prevents you from learning, traveling, reaching out to others, or is jealous of you, rethink the relationship and do not hinder the other person's opportunities and growth in life.
– Laura, 50

If you have to spend your time trying to be popular, you really are not.
– Tom, 45

Don't get involved with boys. Boys are ALL walking hormones as teenagers. The ones who aren't are emo. Who wants an emo husband ten years from now?
– Jen, 33

Never underestimate the power of your mom's advice. It may be hard to hear but chances are the angrier it makes you, the more right she is. Most of the time you'll be glad you grabbed the scarf.
– Gabrielle, 19

I think every girl (especially the pre-teen age) struggles with friendships. I was 10 when we moved to Rhode Island and went to a small Catholic school, similar in size to [the one my daughters go to]. Such a tough age; it seemed everyone around me had their best friends that they had since kindergarten. All I wanted was that one best friend. Despite the fact that I was friends with everyone, I always felt inadequate because I didn't have that bond with that one girl...no girl in particular, just one. It took me years to realize that being friends with everyone, the nerds, the jocks, the theater kids, band kids, punks, preps...everyone...was the best friendships anyone can have. I stress that to my girls all the time. It's so much better to be friends with everyone!

– Melissa, 44

MIND

"Biology gives you a brain. Life turns it into a mind."
— Jeffrey Eugenides, *Middlesex*

"Open your eyes, train your ears, use your head. If a mind you have,
then use it while you can."
— Haruki Murakami, *Hard-Boiled Wonderland and the End of the
World*

If you love math and/or science, talk to an advisor, mentor or someone of the like about pursuing a career in engineering. With women being a minority in the field, and the world constantly engineering new products, it will always be a secure field for you, you'll always be able to find a job, your job will likely be super cool (i.e. picture saying something like "I helped design that prosthetic arm that integrates with the nervous system so the fingers move, just like everyone else!" or "I designed a robot that soldiers use in combat, so they are kept out of the line of fire...I save soldiers' lives!") AND there will likely be cute boys at work. And if math/science/engineering isn't appealing to you, talk to as many different people as possible about potential career paths. Your eyes will be opened to a whole lot more than it is now.

– Darlene, 34

Don't be a follower; think about what you are doing.
– Modia, 40

Think about what you want, set a goal, and map out the steps to get there. Keep at it. You get all ditherry because you don't know what comes next. Look at your plan and work on the next step. And say NO to that stupid boy, and the other one, too. Focus on what makes YOU feel good, happy and productive and keep working towards your goals. And by the way, you look just fine!
– Deborah, 59

I think it is important for young women to be able to support themselves, which includes being able to balance a check point, set up a savings account, use a screw driver and change a flat tire.
– Kim, 45

Listen to everyone around you, but decide for yourself what 'advice' is worthy of following.
– Karen, 64

Allow yourself to get really bored and then, in those down, quiet, boring times, you'll figure out what you really love, what you really want to do, who you really are. If you add too many things in your life, stay too busy, you'll just keep going to the next thing without figuring out what is really important to you.
– Holly, 40

Become as smart as possible and learn to be independent.
– Ford, 64

Be open to learning about everything, choose to follow
only what you believe.
– Karen, 64

Seek out those respected and emulate them.
– Jerry, 67

Stay in school.
– Dave, 44

Be wary of social networks. People are not always what they claim to be, so never give out private information – period - even if you know the person.
- Phil, "at the peak of middle age, and about 25-30 years from retirement"

Make mistakes and take chances but don't forget to learn from them. Regret is the hardest feeling to shake.
– Gabrielle, 19

Try to be a good listener always. God gave us 2 ears and one mouth and sometimes we act like we have 2 mouths, always yapping, and only one ear hardly listening.
– Laura, 50

Learn how to cook, even if it's just simple things. You can save money and time and eat healthier when you are "grown up" if you learn some cooking skills early on. Plus, your Mom and Dad will appreciate it if you can cook every once in a while.
– Sara, 36

You will make mistakes. Just be sure you learn from them. Doesn't matter when...just learn.
I just realized a lesson I learned from a mistake I made with a friend when I was 17. I only figured it out when I was 36.
– Trish, 37

Use your intelligence and don't just trust anyone.
– Modia, 40

Travel wherever you can. Experience other cultures. Eat different food. Try to speak that country's language and not rely on English! You can't understand people from other cultures and the way they think until you have literally been there. There is so much Americans take for granted, but after experiencing other ways of living, we can grow in amazing ways. Travel opens ones one's eyes and mind.
– Lynne, 59

DON'T dummy down for a boy.
– Mary, 64

Get a good education, because that is not only crucial for
doing (or figuring out) what you want to do in life, but it
will also help you to appreciate
what you have wherever you end up.
– Len, 44

Stay in school, study everything, and travel wherever you
can; experience the culture, don't just observe it.
– Karen, 64

Study a language and don't be afraid to explore the world and learn about those who are different from you (you don't have to travel to do this - just be open and interested in learning about how other people live, feel, and experience life). The ability to see things from a different perspective and understand where other people are coming from is probably one of the most important (and hardest) life skills you will ever learn.

- John, 41

Learn from your mistakes.
— Laura, 50

Everything worth having is worth working for. It will not be
easy, but totally worth it.
— Melissa, 32

It's ok to make mistakes. It's not okay to make mistakes
and not learn something from them.
— Sarah, 36

Forgive yourself for not being perfect; no one is.
– Laura, 50

Work hard, be kind.
– Mary, 64

Study hard. Work for every college scholarship you can. Speaking as someone who was blessed with a free ride, I know you do NOT want to saddle yourself with hundreds of thousands of dollars in debt that will take decades to remove from your credit report.

– Jen, 33

You will NEVER regret getting an education; learn as much as you can, whether you think you'll ever use it or not.

- Anonymous

Aim for the stars when it comes to your education. Think you want to be a nurse? What about being a nurse practitioner or a doctor!
– Anonymous

Know what your dreams are
and pursue them with passion.
– Jim, 49

Try your best and
do not worry about what others think of you.
– Tim, 55

If you are ever upset or things aren't easy, take a step back and assess what the real problem is, and realistically how you can fix it. Sitting in a pool of self-pity and tears never gets you anywhere. Wipe your eyes and move on.
– Gabrielle, 19

Always be looking for life's lessons
in all that you do.
– Kevin, 39

Focus on your studies; don't count on anyone else to take
care of you in your adult life.
– Anonymous

Finish your education before you do anything else in life.
It's so much harder to do homework once you have a
mortgage, a spouse and kids to distract you.
– Robin, 42

Work hard and you will succeed.

– Gina, 24

Study hard and learn about things that interest you, even if they aren't cool. Learn to write and speak well.

– Melissa, 44

Travel, explore, learn new things.

– Modia, 40

Trust that life only gets better when you open yourself up
to understand the difficulties as lessons
that will make you stronger.
- Modia, 40

Always choose the *hard* right over the *easy* wrong.
– Sherrie, 53

Learn to be a critical and creative thinker.
– Don, 73

Never give up, things may get tough in life as well as school but never give up because once you do you will only regret it later!

– Kristen, "35 years young"

You can be anything you want to be, no matter what anyone tells you. The key is education and confidence.

– Arnie, 61 ("but feels 39")

Travel every chance you can.
– Mary, 64

You don't lose education!
– Phil, "at the peak of middle age, and about 25-30 years from
retirement"

Fail fast and often. If you are always involved in projects, classes, and groups where you are experiencing success after success, and receiving nothing but praise, you aren't learning and you aren't challenging yourself. Or, WORSE...the teacher believes you cannot succeed and is basically patting you on the head and avoiding wasting time with you. One of the smartest things I did in high school was, when I made 1st chair clarinet in my sophomore year of high school, instead of just enjoying being the best clarinetist in my peer group for 3 years without having to bother practicing or learning anything, I got permission to enroll in chamber music and "clarinet choir" at the local university. Did the 20-somethings give me a lot of crap? Did I feel stupid a lot? Yes and yes. But they were living at home and had day jobs, and when I got to be their age I was supporting myself as a professional musician and living on my own. When I look back, I wished I had challenged myself more like that, in more areas.
– Denise, 43

You don't yet know what you don't know. Keep your mind
open to new experiences, new cultures, new feelings and
decide for yourself!
– Patti, 57

Regarding travel, experience as many cultures as you can.
Live the lessons you learn in doing so.
– Don, 73

Don't react. Just breathe. Breathe again. Think.
Then answer.
– Trish, 37 ("although some days I feel like I'm 14")

Get a PhD (or the highest degree in your field).
– Kim, 52

Travel to different places when you grow up. Traveling gives you not only great memories, but it gives you a sense of adventure and of confidence. It makes you more well-rounded and interesting.
– Anonymous

There are several things you should have and learn to use - learn to fix things, have your own tool kit, learn to change a tire and the oil in your car, learn to write a good cover letter and resume, learn how to fill out a job application and how to handle an interview, get a good, sturdy suitcase for travel, always keep a blanket, water and granola bars in your trunk in winter, learn how to balance your check book, pay attention to your investment accounts and retirement, have a good, trustworthy financial adviser and follow his/her advice, have enough money in savings for 6 months of living expenses, marry someone that you can talk to and who makes you laugh because looks can fade
...always be true to yourself.

– Michele, 52

Don't rely on someone else to take care of you
in the future.
Build your plans around taking care of yourself.
– Robin, 42

Question everything with an open heart and an open mind.
– Elizabeth, 30

Stop obsessing about that one thing! The number on the scale, the size of your hips, your bra size, the space between your teeth, or whatever that one thing is for you. That one thing that makes you unhappy every time you see it in the mirror. You are so much more than that! You are beautiful! You will make a positive impact on the lives of more people than you can even imagine! But, you can only relish in the joy of that, if you love you, in totality, just as you are!

- Karen, 52

You're going to make mistakes. Don't worry about it. Making mistakes says you are trying new things. That means you are learning and growing. Try to arrange your life so that you do what you love; if for some reason that isn't possible, work on learning to love what you do. I truly believe Albert Schweizer's quote that a life led for others is harder, but it is also richer and happier. That being said, balance in life is good. You do not have to say yes to every request; you do not have to be busy all the time; you do not have to be the best at everything; you do not have to be perfect. You are not your grades or your test scores. Don't think you have to learn everything at once or be everything you are going to be all at once. There are plenty of examples of people who developed a new talent or passion at thirty or forty or fifty or sixty. My grandma didn't start water coloring until she was sixty. Now her pictures grace our walls. A good trick, if you can learn it, is to enjoy the questions without worrying about them. Every time you don't get what you want, a whole new world of possibilities opens up. What if you don't get into the school you wanted to get into? Well, then, you'll get into another school where you will maybe discover a whole new side of yourself or you'll meet someone who will become your lifelong friend. It is okay to be smart and beautiful. It is okay to disagree with people. You don't have to be mean about it, but you have as much right to respectfully voice your opinion as anyone else does. You won't always get your own way, but you should make sure you get your way some of the time.

– Elisabeth, 47

Don't slouch - physically or metaphorically.

— Kelli, 48

Happiness is not coincidental. It is made.
You are the only person who can
make you happy.

- Arfe

Save, invest, put aside a portion of any money.
- Andrea, 49

EDUCATION - You can never have enough!
– Kristen, "35 years young"

I would say learn how to balance a check book. From the time you get your very first paycheck, always put 5% or more away. If you wait tables & you bring home $15.00 in tips, it won't kill you to set aside $1.50. Put it in a special bank account or a piggy bank. You won't miss that $1.50. If you do this as a habit, you will become financially secure. Having some money gives you a sense of security, but DO have fun and splurge on yourself (and others) now and then.

– Anonymous

Take every piece of advice you get with a grain of salt. Your life is like no one else's and their experiences won't be the same as your own. Nobody knows everything.

Live your own life.
– Gabrielle, 19

Become comfortable with relativity.
– Don, 73

Follow your true passion....chose a career that will bring you joy each day. Don't be afraid to make a difference and stand up for what you believe in. Money isn't the only reason to choose a job or career.
– Amy, 42

Make YOURSELF PROUD in whatever your do. When facing obstacles of life, does it feel like you made the best decision possible?

— Gordon, 67

Take time to understand yourself and how you work and relate with others. [Understand the] importance of seeking out what you want to do and maybe trying something new that may not be currently available.

— Andrea, 49

Spirit

"Human spirit is the ability to face the uncertainty of the future with curiosity and optimism. It is the belief that problems can be solved, differences resolved.
It is a type of confidence.
And it is fragile. It can be blackened by fear, and superstition."
— Bernard Beckett, *Genesis*

The true measure of a person's character is how she acts when no one is looking and how she acts when the chips are down. Behave with integrity, and no matter what else you lose in life, you will always have that. Always be prepared; but accept that you cannot control life. Something will come along that you do not expect. You're going to make mistakes. Don't worry about it. Making mistakes says you are trying new things. That means you are learning and growing.

– Elisabeth, 47

Don't let other people make your decisions for you or even let them have sway over your choices.
– Gabrielle, 19

Stand up to wrong doers and do what is right.
Defend the weak,
help the needy,
and support the strong.
– Modia, 40

It is important for girls to have self-respect and to believe they are capable of anything they choose. They need not be dependent on others for a sense of self-worth. These attributes can help minimize negative situations they may otherwise experience.

– Kim, 45

Remember that you are much stronger than you give yourself credit for,
and more capable than you may think.

– Laura, 28

I think as a young girl, I never fully understood my own empowerment. That I had a voice and what I had to say was important. As teens we all just wanted to fit in, feeling like standing out or standing up for something not popular may put you out of the "crowd". Being afraid that your "friends" may cast you out for your opinions or if you're "different" is a real fear for teens. I got past that pretty quick and realized that running with the popular crowd wasn't as important as I thought! Once I felt free of that, my true friends were still there and so was my real empowerment as a young woman.

– Marcia, 52

You have the power to be a beautiful person; it has nothing to do with how you look or dress, it's all in how you carry yourself and treat others.
– Melissa, 32

Find a strong, positive, female role model as a mentor and coach who can help you surface your internal motivators, develop/support the solidifying of your self-confidence, and encourage you to explore all the opportunities life has to offer.
– Rita, 67

Participate in our democracy. Stand up, speak out. Embrace opportunities to make our world a better place - even the small ones.
– Elizabeth, 30

Do the thing that scares you.
– Laura, 28

Happiness is a choice.
Tonda, 47

Teenage girls shouldn't allow their insecurities to hold them back. They need to be satisfied with themselves and find their specialness to achieve their goals in life.
– Lee, 43

Be yourself; everyone else is already taken!
– Karen, 64

Confidence.
– Hadeel, 31

Have 20 seconds of courage. We are all scared, nervous, afraid in different situations in life, but if you can initially have 20 seconds of courage, you can handle anything!
– Linda, 50

As cheesy as it sounds, respect yourself because others (friends, guys, teachers, peers, classmates) will follow suit. If you stick up for yourself, there's less chance that they will walk all over you. People respect people that respect themselves. If you're not going to take yourself seriously, who will?
– Gabrielle, 19

You are cool now and you always will be.
- Anonymous

Work every day to be the very best version of yourself you can be, not who you think everyone else wants you to be. You are the only "you" there is.
– Sara, 36

Don't try to grow up too fast. Being a kid, I always wanted to be an adult because it looked like so much more fun. It isn't; enjoy your youth!

– Lisa, 37

Don't rush your teen years away, enjoy every moment possible; once you become an adult you will wish at times that you were a kid again.
– Melissa, 32

Advocate for yourself.
- Anonymous

Do not let anyone define who you are and learn to grow in love with who you are because if you do believe in yourself, you can do anything.
– Lesley, 67

Be true to yourself.
– Marty, 56

You are beautiful, and lovely, and worth fighting for.
– Jim, 49

Travel now...there will never be "more time" or "more
money" later.
– Robin, 42

Always value yourself and never settle.
– Gina, 24

Always respect yourself.
– Jim, 49

Learn to have confidence in yourself and your decisions.

Stand for yourself and feel sure of yourself;
[your confidence] will shine through,
help you make friends,
and open wonderful opportunities.
The confidence in your decisions will help you stand for
yourself in tough situations.
– Sandy, 67

Life is a journey, enjoy it, feel it, learn always and love and
respect all those you meet.

– Laura, 50

Take a deep breath.
There are always bullies out there. You'll have to take your
knocks. Stick to your school work and ignore the negativity.
Cry if you have to.

– Jen, 33

Love and Respect are the most important things in life
which we learn in our Faith. Believe in God; you have been
blessed and you can always rely on Him. Always speak to
God and thank HIM for all your blessings,
even the little ones.

– Laura, 50

Love yourself. Remember there is only one of you in this world.
– Arfe

Learn to be kind and make good decisions from a very early age.
– Denise, 42

People who insult you are jealous or insecure (most times both). Let their words roll off you and keep on walking.
– Gabrielle, 19

Never give up.

– Kim, 52

Regardless of what you have come to believe there really is
nothing wrong with you.
You are likable,
you are beautiful
and you can accomplish anything you put your mind to.
– Michele, 42

As a friend's mom used to say, "Life ain't no dress
rehearsal."

- Lee, 42

Follow your heart and desires...
travel,
have fun and experience as much of life
as you can,
take music lessons, foreign language, art,
dance...
learn about other countries...
where your family came from....

When we open ourselves up to new
experiences we grow so much.
We become fearless in some ways and learn
our boundaries and limitations in
other ways!
No matter what you do or where you go,
find the joy and beauty that is offered to us
everyday!

Laugh....
– Stephanie, 39 ("or 21")

Be who you are and who you would want people to be to you, but don't stress too much when they don't reciprocate; you can't control others actions...
only your own.
– Melissa, 32

Believe in yourself,

you're only limited by your imagination and any unwillingness to risk failure.
– Karen, 64

Decide what makes you happy, and do those things.
- Anonymous

Be true and honest to yourself and others. Believe in
yourself. Try new things that you know are safe and
morally correct.
- Laura, 46

Remember to be the best person you can be
by being yourself and truthful to your heart.
– Kevin, 39

Respect and accept yourself, because if you don't, no one else will either. People will constantly make fun of you, bully you and poke fun at you, but if you can accept yourself for who you are, people cannot use your flaws against you.
- Lauren, 20

Always be authentic; you will never truly be happy pretending to be someone you are not.
–Tina, 45

Never rely on anyone! BE INDEPENDENT; this will be very valuable later in life when you are single and don't need someone else for anything. Independence and learning how to do that is so important, you can gain so much confidence as a woman when you are independent.
– Kristen, "35 years young"

Each of us gets one shot; there are no dress rehearsals.
– Don, 73

Listen to your inner voice.
– Marty, 56

Nothing in life is more guaranteed or permanent than God's love for you. Love Him back in any small way you know how to do. He is there for you in the middle of the night, middle of a test, middle of an awkward situation with friends, and then be thankful and kind to the ones He has given you here on earth to love you. In five years you will look back and realize He guided you through many challenges.
– Merri, 58

Always be yourself.
– Tim, 55

Look closely at what are the things you choose to do a lot, what you like to do the most, what makes you happiest when you do it, what you want to do more of, and what you think you do well and may hear that from others. Make plans to pursue a life and career that is based on those. You will be happiest, most creative, and do most good for yourself and those you love by living a life that incorporates a good deal of time and freedom to do what you like, are good at and want to do more of, rather than a life of what you think you should do, what others say you should do, or what minimizes what you hold as important.
– Stephen, 65

Don't ever lose your sense of humor...life is just much easier to bear, and there will be time when all you can do is hold on. That's when you have to still have your humor help you get through the day!
– Sue, 67

Nothing is so far gone that you cannot interrupt it, change it, maybe even stop it. You just need to believe you can.
- Sherrie, 53

You need to be sure to listen to the little voice inside you that is desperately trying to be heard and give you direction. There are so many people in your life who are offering their opinions about who you should be, how you should look, or how you should act. Most of them are very well meaning, but in a lot of cases, they want you to be someone who makes them feel better about themselves; not be the best "you" that you can be. That voice will help you choose the best path to help you reach your goals. It is so easy to get off track, but if you are true to yourself, you are more likely to end up somewhere that makes you feel happy, satisfied and complete. Every decision you make, when you follow your heart, will make your journey that much more rewarding in the end!

– Karen, 48

Be smart.
Be assertive.
Be sweet.
Be beautiful.
Be plain.
Whomever you are or want to become, be
yourself.

Like singing.
Like trucks.
Like math.
Like flowers.
Like cake.
Whomever you are or want to become, like
yourself.

Love carefully.
Love deeply.
Love warmly.
Love thoughtfully.
Love truthfully.
Whomever you are or want to become, love
yourself.
– Heath, 48

Don't let fear of failure hold you back; failures are the
stepping stones to success.
– Don, 73

Trust in God.
– Tim, 55

Avoid all the drama.
– Justin, 13

Nothing is ever as bad as it seems and I promise you one day it won't mean that much to you. You'll change, grow and understand, but right now just keep your head up and look to the future; enjoy your youth 'cause you'll never have it again.
– Kelly, 22

Stay strong! It's worth it!
– Katie, 36

No matter how rough it may seem, your inner knowing never lies. Trust your authentic voice and be who you are, no matter what they say.
– Brie, 36

Trust and listen to your inner voice, stay in
touch with it, and run when it tells you to.
– Modia, 40

Do YOUR personal BEST at everything you do.
– Terri, 51

Never lose your sense of humor.
- Anonymous

Never do the wrong thing for the "right" reason.
- Anonymous

Be true to yourself and go with your first instinct. Ask yourself, "Would I be embarrassed or let anyone down if I was caught," before doing anything "naughty".
- Anonymous

Be true to yourself. Don't be afraid to have your own voice and your own opinions. The teenage years can be the most difficult.
Life really does get easier after high school.
– Keri, 56

Always do the right thing. No one could fault you for that.
- Anonymous

The things that seem so important and overwhelming will take a new shape and perspective as you get older and really won't matter. Don't beat yourself up when you make mistakes; you will eventually be able to look back and see their lessons and how you've grown from them.
- Erin, 42

Think about the things you value most in life. Once you decide, try to always do things that are in line with your values, even if that means not pleasing everyone. You will be happier in the long run.
– Stacey, 26

Regarding career, do what you love.
The rest will take care of itself.
– Don, 73

That no matter what they have, to learn to love and accept themselves as is. After they get that down, DREAM BIG; anything you work hard for will pay off.
– Lori, 43

You and only you are in control of your life. Don't ever let anyone tell you can't do something because you are a woman...the only limitations you have are the ones you place on yourself...don't let society dictate your success or happiness.

Also leave home...see the world and travel...discover who you really are. Then, if it is right for you, come home...find the perfect place to be you.

Always be true to yourself. It is hard sometimes to be that independent thinker and doer...never compromise who you are for any one...march to your own drummer and never let anyone change your beat...being a woman is not always easy, but as you grow up you will become stronger than you ever imaged anyone could...it is all inside of you.

– Michele, 50

The most beautiful thing you can be is yourself. It took me a long time to figure that out and I wish someone had told me that when I was younger.

– Amber, 28

Be proud of how different you feel.
You don't need to fit in the cookie cutter.
You'll be ok.

– Huda, 31

"Be who you are and say what you feel because those who mind don't matter and those who matter won't mind" from Dr. Seuss.

- Laura, 28

That you have to stand up for yourself, and be true to yourself. That you can be respectful and polite to an elder, but also defend yourself. Example if a teacher is putting you down, you can simply state that you are capable. That when friends are saying that you are fat, are not good enough that you respond with, "Well, that is your opinion" and walk away. There is so much that goes on with these girls, but they really have to know the difference between standing up for themselves, positive image and what isn't simply talking back and being a tattle tale.

– Anonymous

I would say, "To thine self be true". Don't let friends, teachers, principals, family dictate who you want to become. Also, you are allowed to make mistakes. These mistakes do not and will not define you. I encourage you to try new things even though you may be scared or nervous. Have courage to expand your thinking and skill sets by trying new things.

– Kristin, 27

Remember that things in life will change, people will change and you will change. Always try to understand yourself, those around you and your time in life as fluid and in motion instead of good or bad, hard or easy. Be in touch with not only the 'what' of this change, but the 'why' and you will be able to move forward and create and find peace, love and happiness, even when changing small or larger parts of your life experience. The goal is to always be the 'you' you know and want to be for yourself as well as for others.

– Stephen, 65

Travel. Make friends with people from cultures different than your own and be curious about what life is like for them.
– Laura, 28

Treat yourself with kindness, always.
- Patty, 32

You are valuable, and don't sell yourself cheap.
– Modia, 40

Keep God close to your heart. This time will be filled with many why's and WHY NOT 's and though your answers probably will not come in the quick fashion you expect, please give your questions to God as honestly as you can and he will provide! When words fail you, a good Our Father or Hail Mary will work wonders.

– Kara, 32

God has made you special and unique.
– Jim, 49

Do what makes YOU happy, not anyone else! At the end of the day it is YOU walking this road. Others may walk it with you, but no one can walk it for you.

– Jess, 31

Take time to be young and silly; you have your whole life to be an adult! But still be responsible for yourself and your own actions.

– Gina, 24

Believe in yourself.
– Modia, 40

The only feelings that you need to take responsibility for are your own. It's all too easy to take responsibility for the feelings of your friends and family. Rather than worrying about how others feel towards your words or actions, you should look inward and decide how you feel about those words or actions. Can you stand behind what you said or did with conviction, pride or justification? If so, you have no reason to feel bad. On the other hand, if you are embarrassed, sad, or frustrated by your words or actions, you need to take the opportunity to learn from your behavior, so you don't repeat the same mistakes over and over again.

– Karen, 48

Something I didn't realize until my early 30's but surely wish I had this understanding during the most difficult years. I call it my pillars of strength. All the negatives in my life I hold very high. The sorrow, hurt, failure, pain, rejection, etc., I use them as a pillar to hold me up higher and stronger. If we never experience sadness, we can't acknowledge and appreciate happiness. If we are never hurt, we won't identify with pleasure. If we never fail, we can't appreciate success to its fullest extent. Every time a negative is repeated, we get hurt again, fail again; it just makes that pillar stronger. So instead of pushing down these negatives, hold them close as a reminder that where there is pain, there is pleasure, failure – success, hate – love, etc., etc.

– Melissa, 44

When God was walking through His warehouse of potential
people, He stopped and took you from the shelf; so, you
truly are a special selection, made to
make the world blessed.
– Bob, 66

Don't let others define who you are! Regardless of what
you have done with your life in the past, today is a new day
and you can be who you want to be.
– Melissa, 32

Love yourself.

There truly is no one exactly like you.

It might take you a while to find your true
place in life, but never stop seeking,
never stop learning
and never stop loving.
– Kara, 32

Final Thoughts

Over the year it took to receive the initial responses, I was very excited about this project. After it was initially rejected by three publishing companies, I ended putting it away in a drawer, periodically feeling sad that the wealth of wisdom and insight within its pages wouldn't be shared. After reading Elizabeth Gilbert's book *Big Magic*, I decided to put the words out there, with my goal to give a copy to each of my daughters to help guide their journeys. The thought of bringing life back to this project inspired me to ask for more contributions and then to finally embark on self-publishing this book.

During those years, I had time to reflect on the power of the thoughts which were shared. As I said in the Preface, this project originally began to offer advice for young women on the verge of adulthood. But when a childhood friend of mine, father to two boys and a girl, pointed out that much of the advice offered could also be shared with his sons (thanks, Eddie!), I began looking at the words shared and realized the much of the advice could be offered to anyone...at any time...throughout their life.

I will share the book with my sons, to offer them some of the insights for their own lives, and to help them understand some of the experiences for the girls and women in their life. I will certainly share the book with my daughters and can only hope they use some of the words to guide them as they traverse the challenges of becoming women. As I was re-reading the early drafts, I shared with one of my friends her own words, during a difficult time in her marriage, hoping that she would find strength from her own voice. And for myself, I have found comfort in the advice from those who contributed. Whether to know others experienced the same when they were growing up, or to know that the advice I have offered to my children (among eye rolls or sighs on their part) are not unique and are significant, or simply to inspire me to look for ways to change and grow even as an adult, this book has afforded an opportunity for the collective wisdom of the Village to be shared.

It is amazing what powerful words were offered by those who contributed to *Voices*. I hope more people consider adding their thoughts to this project via the survey found at https://www.surveymonkey.com/s/TGP9B86 or on Facebook at https://www.facebook.com/VoicesfromtheVillage?ref_type= bookmark.

- Robin

Made in the USA
Charleston, SC
26 October 2016